IBH 90-Day Guided

AWARENESS JOURNAL

Your Path to *Personal Growth & Empowerment*

Interior by JJAC Graphics, LLC

Cover Design by JJAC Graphics, LLC

Editorial Direction by Anita Willis

Printed in the United States

ISBN: 979-8-9855076-2-1

 info@builditbeyond.com

 www.BuildItBeyond.com

 build_it beyond_anitawillis

 Anita Dawn Willis

 Anita Willis IBH

 @builditbeyond

THIS JOURNAL BELONGS TO

_____

YOUR TIME OF ELEVATION AND AWARENESS

Your IBH New Year Guided Awareness Journal is not just a tool for reflection; it's supports a self-directed transformational companion for women on the journey to personal growth. It encourages the practice of affirming care, resilience, and a grounded sense of self, while aligning the user's life with their deeper values and spiritual truth. By integrating the practices of gratitude, self-love, growth, and intentional living, the journal encourages the pursuit of a balanced, meaningful life that reflects hope, empowerment, and a bright future. In no way is it therapy, formal consultation, or professional advice, but as information and entertainment purposes at the sole discretion of the reader.

Embark on a transformative journey with the "IBH 90-Day Awareness Journal: Your Path to Personal Growth and Empowerment." This first installment in a groundbreaking series is more than just a journal; it's a beacon for women seeking to navigate the waters of self improvement and personal enlightenment. Crafted to inspire affirming care, resilience, and a profound connection with one's inner values and spiritual truths, this guided awareness journal is your companion in fostering gratitude, self-love, growth, and a life of intention. It's designed to guide you toward a harmonious balance, empowering you to build a future filled with hope and empowerment.

While not a substitute for professional advice, this journal is a powerful tool for information, entertainment, and self-directed transformation, inviting you to explore the depths of your being and align your life with your deepest aspirations. There are 4 in the IBH Awareness Journal Series.

This journal is the companion to the book

**"BUILD IT BEYOND:
FROM A DREAM TO A VISION FOR YOUR LIFE".**

BUILD IT BEYOND
From New Year Resolutions to Guided Awareness

Here's an outline of the informational opportunities for someone using the journal:

1. ENHANCED SELF-AWARENESS

Expected Outcome:
Users will develop a deeper understanding of their thoughts, emotions, and behaviors, allowing them to become more in tune with their internal experiences.

Impact:
- Increased emotional intelligence, enabling better self-regulation and awareness of how actions and reactions affect relationships.

- A greater ability to identify and break patterns of negative self-talk or limiting beliefs.

- Enhanced clarity in understanding personal values, purpose, and long-term goals.

2. IMPROVED SELF-FORGIVENESS AND HEALING

Expected Outcome:
The journal will encourage users to engage in self-forgiveness practices, facilitating emotional release and personal healing.

Impact:
- Reduction in feelings of guilt, shame, and regret, replaced by self-

compassion and acceptance.

- A more positive and healthier self-concept, boosting overall well-being and emotional resilience.

- Healing of emotional wounds, leading to more peace and self-acceptance.

3. CULTIVATION OF RESILIENCE AND PERSONAL GROWTH

Expected Outcome:
Through daily prompts and reflections, users will focus on developing a growth mindset, seeing challenges as opportunities to learn and grow.

Impact:
- Increased resilience when faced with adversity, including better coping mechanisms for stress and setbacks.

- An empowered mindset where failures are seen as learning experiences, not personal shortcomings.

- A deeper connection to one's potential, encouraging continuous personal growth and transformation.

4. STRENGTHENED SPIRITUAL AND MENTAL FOCUS

Expected Outcome:
Regular spiritual practices through prayer and reflection can support mental clarity, focus, and alignment with personal and spiritual goals.

Impact:
- Promote a sense of peace and inner balance, as users integrate spirituality into their daily life.

- Enhanced focus on present moments and priorities, reducing distractions and improving productivity.

- A stronger sense of purpose and connection to a higher power, enriching personal spirituality.

5. BETTER COMMUNICATION AND RELATIONSHIP BUILDING

Expected Outcome:
As users practice self-awareness and emotional regulation, they can develop better communication skills, especially in relationships.

Encourage:
- Improved interpersonal skills, including more open, honest, and compassionate communication.

- Strengthened relationships with family, friends, and colleagues as a result of emotional intelligence and vulnerability.

- Reduced conflicts and misunderstandings due to clearer communication and empathy.

6. ENCOURAGE SELF-LOVE AND ACCEPTANCE

Expected Outcome:
By regularly practicing self-compassion and acknowledging personal achievements and strengths, users will experience a boost in self-love and self-worth.

Impact:
- Heightened confidence and self-esteem, allowing users to take bold actions aligned with their personal values.

- A reduction in negative self-judgment and a growing acceptance of one's flaws and imperfections.

- Greater appreciation of one's unique qualities and a deeper connection with self.

7. ENCOURAGE HEALTHIER BOUNDARIES AND EMOTIONAL PROTECTION

Expected Outcome:
The journal encourages setting and maintaining healthy boundaries, promoting emotional and physical well-being.

Impact:
- Reduced burnout and emotional exhaustion by learning to say no and prioritize self-care.

- Increased assertiveness in protecting one's emotional and mental space, leading to healthier, more balanced relationships.

- A more empowered approach to handling stress and external pressures, by learning to establish boundaries.

- A more positive and healthier self-concept, boosting overall well-being and emotional resilience.

- Healing of emotional wounds, leading to more peace and self-acceptance.

BUILD IT BEYOND
With Intentional Living

1. PROMOTE A POSITIVE FUTURE OUTLOOK AND INTENTIONAL LIVING

Encouraged Outcome:
Users will set clear intentions and actionable goals, creating a hopeful vision for their future and actively working towards it.

Impact:
- A sense of purpose and clarity in life, leading to actionable steps toward long-term aspirations.

- Greater alignment between daily actions and overarching life goals, leading to a more fulfilling and intentional lifestyle.

- A positive, optimistic view of the future, nurtured by consistent reflection and goal-setting.

2. DEEPER GRATITUDE AND MINDFUL LIVING

Encouraged Outcome:
The journal will encourage users to adopt a mindset of gratitude, focusing on appreciating the present and the small blessings in life.

Impact:
- Increased sense of joy, contentment, and fulfillment through daily practices of gratitude.

- More mindful and purposeful living, where users are present in each moment and aware of the blessings around them.

- A more positive, abundant mindset, leading to better mental and emotional health.

4.   HOLISTIC WELLNESS AND BALANCE

Encouraged Outcome:
By integrating spiritual, emotional, and mental practices into their routine, users will experience overall wellness and a sense of balance in their lives.

Impact:
- Improved mental health and emotional stability through consistent self-care practices.

- A harmonious balance between work, relationships, and personal well-being, reducing stress and promoting life satisfaction.

- Greater ability to achieve holistic wellness, where spiritual, emotional, and physical health work together to create a fulfilling life.

Dear sister, take a moment and review pages 4-8 again Write in the space below what stands out. You'll thank me in 90 days when this is no longer a dream, but a vision for your life.

_____

_____

_____

_____

_____

Month 1

Cultivating Self-Awareness and Emotional Intelligence

The 3-month IBH New Year Guided "Awareness" Journal blends the core concepts of self-awareness, healthy relationships, and growth after disappointment. The journal is designed to guide you through practices of reflection, mindfulness, and intentional living to foster a deeper connection with yourself and others as you enter the new year.

A New Dawn

Embracing Self-Forgiveness and Growth

This reimagined story follows Maya, a woman of color, through her journey of self-forgiveness, growth, and healing after years of navigating the complexities of life challenges, poor decisions and expectations.

The Weight of the Past

Maya sat by the window, watching the early morning sun stretch its golden rays across the horizon. The world outside was waking up—cars on the street, birds in the trees—but in the quiet of her apartment, she felt an overwhelming sense of stillness. Her gaze drifted to the stack of unopened job applications on the coffee table, the emails unanswered, and the old journal beside her that had once captured the dreams of her younger self.

Growing up as a Black woman in a world where opportunities always seemed more distant, Maya had learned early that she had to work harder than most to prove herself. Her mother had drilled it into her: "You have to be better than them to be seen as equal." And so, she pushed herself, striving for perfection, trying to overcome the barriers that were set before her by the weight of systemic racism.

Yet, despite all the effort, the disappointments kept piling up. Maya's hard work seemed to go unnoticed, her voice often drowned out in rooms where she didn't belong. The subtle racism she encountered daily had chipped away at her self-worth, leaving her wondering if she would ever truly succeed.

Sitting there in the stillness of her apartment, Maya felt a familiar knot of frustration tighten in her chest. Why bother? she thought. But as the sunlight warmed her skin, she felt a tiny flicker of something new—a whisper, faint yet powerful, You are enough.

It wasn't the first time she'd heard that voice, but this time it felt different. It felt true. She knew it was time to learn to forgive herself—for all the times she had let self-doubt win, for all the dreams she had given up on. Maya had spent too many years letting the world tell her what she couldn't be. It was time to listen to what she could be.

The Healing Path Begins

A few days later, Maya found herself sitting in her favorite park, perched on a weathered bench beneath a tall oak tree. It had always been her place of clarity, a space where the noise of the world seemed to fade. As she closed her eyes, taking in a deep, grounding breath, she reflected on the years she had spent burdened by guilt, anger, and regret.

I've carried this weight for far too long, she thought. It's time to let it go.

Maya remembered reading a passage in a book the night before: "Self-forgiveness is not a destination, but a journey—a daily choice to release the past so you can create something new." At first, she didn't believe it, but as the words resonated deeper, she realized that this was exactly what she needed. She didn't have to carry the weight of every injustice, every setback. What would it feel like to truly forgive myself? she wondered. What if I stopped seeing my mistakes as failures and started viewing them as opportunities to grow?

In that moment, Maya made a promise to herself: she would no longer allow the failures of the past, or the prejudices of others, to define her. Forgiveness wasn't about condoning what had happened to her—it was about freeing herself from the anger and disappointment that had held her back for so long.

The journey to self-forgiveness was not an easy one, but it was the beginning of something new—a rebirth of hope and possibility.

The Power of Compassion and Growth

In the following weeks, Maya began to approach her life with a renewed sense of growth. She wasn't perfect, but every time she faced a challenge, she made a conscious effort to see it as an opportunity to evolve, not a setback. She started changing her inner dialogue. Instead of letting thoughts of inadequacy consume her, she began to tell herself, I am not defined by my past. I am capable of growth. She also worked hard to practice compassion, not just for others, but for herself. Maya had always extended kindness to friends and family, but she realized she had never shown herself the same grace. Her mistakes, her doubts—she carried them around like heavy chains, refusing to forgive herself.

One sunny afternoon, while walking through her neighborhood, Maya saw children laughing in the park, elders chatting on their porches. She smiled at their joy and felt a shift in her heart. If I can be kind to them, why can't I be kind to myself? She decided to extend that same compassion inward.

And with that, a subtle change began. Each day, Maya found herself letting go of a little more of the burden. She practiced patience with herself, acknowledging that growth took time, and that healing was a process. Slowly, the weight of self-judgment began to lift.

Reaffirming Commitment to Herself and the Future

One afternoon, Maya met her best friend, Kayla at their favorite coffee shop. Kayla had been her rock for years—someone who had always been there to listen, to offer support, without ever judging her. Today, Maya felt a deep sense of openness between them, a desire to share more of her heart.

"Girl," Kayla said, sipping her coffee, "You've been glowing lately. What's going on with you?"

Maya hesitated but then found herself opening up. For the first time in a long time, she spoke openly about her journey—the racism she had experienced, the emotional toll it had taken, and the work she was doing to forgive herself. She shared how she had been learning to accept her imperfections and let go of the past.

Kayla nodded in understanding, her eyes soft with empathy. "You've always been resilient, Maya. But you don't have to carry that weight alone anymore. You deserve to let it go, to release those past wounds."

Maya smiled, feeling a wave of relief washing over her. She had never been one to share her deepest struggles so openly, but in that moment, she realized how freeing it was to communicate honestly. The support from her best friend only solidified her belief that healthy relationships were built on trust, vulnerability, and understanding.

Reaffirming Commitment to Herself and the Future

As the weeks turned into months, Maya continued to put into practice what she had learned. She focused on living in the present, appreciating the small moments—like the warmth of the sun on her face, the laughter of her nieces and nephews, the satisfaction of a good cup of coffee. She worked on setting healthy boundaries, saying no when she needed to and putting her own well-being first. One evening, after a long day of work, Maya sat by her window, looking out over the city. The skyline glimmered in the soft light, and she felt a quiet sense of peace settle in her heart. For the first time in a long time, she wasn't worried about the future. She knew there were still challenges ahead, but she had finally begun to see herself not as a victim of circumstance, but as a woman capable of achieving everything she dreamed.

She thought about the lessons she had learned—the importance of self-forgiveness, compassion, open communication, and a hopeful outlook on the future. The road hadn't been easy, but Maya had walked it with resilience, courage, and a renewed sense of purpose.

With a smile on her face and gratitude in her heart, Maya whispered to herself, The future is mine to create.

And for the first time, she truly believed it.

CHANGE YOUR MIND, YOU CHANGE YOUR CHOICES

Here are **10** thought and mindset practices that can help power healthy, loving relationships after disappointment:

01

Embrace Forgiveness (Self and Others)

Let go of past hurts by forgiving both yourself and others. Holding onto resentment can hinder healing and prevent you from building a loving, supportive relationship again.

02

Adopt a Perspective of Growth

View disappointment as a learning opportunity rather than a setback. Focus on what can be learned from the experience and how it can contribute to growth within yourself and your relationship.

03

Practice Compassion

Cultivate empathy for yourself and others. Understanding that everyone experiences disappointment and has their own challenges fosters healing and strengthens emotional connection.

04

Communicate Openly and Honestly

Be open about your feelings and expectations. Honest communication allows both partners to understand each other better and work through disappointments together.

05

Cultivate Patience

Healing takes time. Be patient with yourself and your partner as you both navigate through the emotions of disappointment and rebuild trust.

Focus on the Present

06 Release the grip of past disappointments by focusing on the present moment. Being fully engaged in the here and now helps create positive experiences and reduces the power of past hurts.

Practice Gratitude

07 Shift your focus from disappointment to gratitude. Acknowledging the positive aspects of your relationship helps to restore hope and appreciation for each other.

Set Healthy Boundaries

08 Define and respect boundaries that promote emotional safety. After disappointment, boundaries are crucial in rebuilding trust and ensuring both partners feel secure and valued.

Reaffirm Your Commitment

09 Renew your dedication to the relationship. Reaffirming your commitment to your partner and the relationship, even in times of disappointment, strengthens the bond and fosters emotional resilience.

Cultivate a Positive, Hopeful Outlook

10 Maintain optimism about the future. By focusing on hope and the potential for renewal, you create a mindset where healing and love can flourish, even after difficult times.

INTENTION

These practices help to transform disappointment into an opportunity for deeper connection, mutual healing, and a more resilient, loving relationship.

UNDERSTAND THE
VALUE OF YOUR VALUE

Here's an outline of **20** thought and mindset practices centered around "self-awareness" that can help improve interdependence, community, and collaboration for a healthy, satisfying lifestyle:

Embrace Radical Self-Honesty

01 Practice transparency with yourself. Acknowledge your strengths, weaknesses, and areas for growth, leading to more authentic connections.

Cultivate Emotional Intelligence

02 Understand and manage your emotions and be empathetic towards others. This helps create deeper, more compassionate relationships.

Practice Active Listening

03 Focus on truly understanding others' perspectives. Listening without judgment fosters better communication and stronger collaboration.

Recognize Your Values

04 Clarify and align your decisions with your core values. This creates a stable foundation for making choices that benefit you and your community.

Mindful Reflection

05 Regularly take time for self-reflection to evaluate your actions, thoughts, and feelings. This increases emotional awareness and growth.

Develop a Growth Mindset

06 Believe that you can improve through effort and learning. Embrace challenges as opportunities for personal development and community contribution.

Recognize the Interconnectedness of All

07

Understand that your actions impact others. Viewing life as interconnected promotes a sense of collective responsibility and collaboration.

Practice Self-Compassion

08

Be kind to yourself in moments of failure or imperfection. This nurtures resilience and helps you contribute positively to relationships and community.

Create Boundaries with Love

09

Establish healthy boundaries that respect your needs and others'. Clear boundaries foster mutual respect and prevent burnout in relationships.

Acknowledge and Overcome Biases

10

Recognize your implicit biases to foster inclusivity and understanding. This opens the door to meaningful connections across diverse perspectives.

Engage in Solution-Oriented Thinking

11

Focus on solutions rather than problems. Adopting a problem-solving mindset can lead to collective action and a more harmonious lifestyle.

Develop the Practice of Gratitude

12

Regularly express gratitude for yourself, others, and the opportunities you have. Gratitude enhances satisfaction in life and promotes positive relationships.

Foster Accountability

13

Hold yourself accountable for your actions and their impact. This encourages trust and mutual respect in both personal and professional environments.

Embrace Vulnerability

14

Be willing to show your true self, imperfections and all. Vulnerability fosters deeper emotional connections and allows for more authentic collaboration.

15
Engage in Collaborative Goal-Setting

Involve others in setting goals and making decisions. Collaborative goal-setting strengthens bonds and aligns efforts for mutual growth.

16
Promote Active Positivity

Cultivate a mindset of optimism and possibility. Positive thinking helps motivate not just yourself but also inspires and supports others.

17
Honor Diversity of Thought

Value differing perspectives as a source of strength. This mindset encourages open dialogue and collaborative problem-solving.

18
Accept the Flow of Change

Acknowledge and adapt to change with flexibility. This mindset helps build resilience, allowing you to collaborate effectively in ever-changing circumstances.

19
Cultivate Patience

Practice patience with yourself and others. Recognizing that growth and collaboration take time enhances the long-term sustainability of relationships.

20
Commit to Continuous Self-Improvement

Never stop learning about yourself and others. A commitment to ongoing self-awareness and personal development enhances your contributions to the community and fosters lifelong collaboration.

INTENTION & ACTION

These practices, when consistently applied, will enhance self-awareness, promote healthier interdependence, and lead to more collaborative and fulfilling relationships and communities.

Week 1

EMBRACE RADICAL SELF-HONESTY

Weekly Challenge

Choose one area to deepen your practice: radical self-honesty, emotional intelligence, compassion, or open communication. Set a challenge that pushes you to grow in that area.

Prompt

Reflect on a moment when you've been less than honest with yourself. How did this impact your decisions or relationships? What truths are you ready to acknowledge now?

_____

_____

_____

_____

_____

_____

_____

"I am ready to face my truths with compassion and clarity."

ACTION

Write down three things about yourself that you've avoided facing.
Choose one to address this week.

1. _____
_____
_____

2. _____
_____
_____

3. _____
_____

BREATHE

Take a moment for thoughtful meditation as you
begin this journey and imagine more!

https://youtu.be/JTLN4G5FIe8

PRAYER FOR SELF-FORGIVENESS AND HEALING

Scripture Reference

"For I will restore health to you, and your wounds I will heal, declares the Lord." - Jeremiah 30:17

Prayer Point

Begin each day with a prayer for self-forgiveness and healing. Acknowledge the emotional burdens you carry and ask for divine help in releasing them.

Prayer

"Dear God, I come before You with a heart that seeks healing. I forgive myself for the times I have doubted my worth and allowed my past to define me. Please heal my emotional wounds, renew my spirit, and help me embrace the present moment with peace. Guide me to release any guilt, anger, or pain that I may be carrying and fill me with Your love and grace. Amen."

Activation Tip

As you wash your hands, visualize the cleansing of your spirit, letting go of past hurts and welcoming healing.

DAY 1

Morning Intention:

What is my intention for today? How will I contribute to my well-being and the well-being of others?

_____

_____

_____

Midday Check-in:

What emotions am I experiencing? What can I do to center myself?

_____

_____

_____

Evening Reflection:

What did I learn today? What did I do to honor myself and others?

_____

_____

_____

DAY 2

Morning Intention:

What is my intention for today? How will I contribute to my well-being and the well-being of others?

_____

_____

_____

Midday Check-in:

What emotions am I experiencing? What can I do to center myself?

_____

_____

_____

Evening Reflection:

What did I learn today? What did I do to honor myself and others?

_____

_____

_____

DAY 3

Morning Intention:

What is my intention for today? How will I contribute to my well-being and the well-being of others?

_____

_____

_____

Midday Check-in:

What emotions am I experiencing? What can I do to center myself?

_____

_____

_____

Evening Reflection:

What did I learn today? What did I do to honor myself and others?

_____

_____

_____

DAY 4

Morning Intention:

What is my intention for today? How will I contribute to my well-being and the well-being of others?

_____

_____

_____

Midday Check-in:

What emotions am I experiencing? What can I do to center myself?

_____

_____

_____

Evening Reflection:

What did I learn today? What did I do to honor myself and others?

_____

_____

_____

DAY 5

Morning Intention:

What is my intention for today? How will I contribute to my well-being and the well-being of others?

_____

_____

_____

Midday Check-in:

What emotions am I experiencing? What can I do to center myself?

_____

_____

_____

Evening Reflection:

What did I learn today? What did I do to honor myself and others?

_____

_____

_____

DAY 6

Morning Intention:

What is my intention for today? How will I contribute to my well-being and the well-being of others?

_____

_____

_____

Midday Check-in:

What emotions am I experiencing? What can I do to center myself?

_____

_____

_____

Evening Reflection:

What did I learn today? What did I do to honor myself and others?

_____

_____

_____

DAY 7

Morning Intention:

What is my intention for today? How will I contribute to my well-being and the well-being of others?

_____

_____

_____

Midday Check-in:

What emotions am I experiencing? What can I do to center myself?

_____

_____

_____

Evening Reflection:

What did I learn today? What did I do to honor myself and others?

_____

_____

_____

Your Thoughts

UNDERSTANDING
YOUR VALUES

Weekly Challenge

Choose one area to deepen your practice: radical self-honesty, emotional intelligence, compassion, or open communication. Set a challenge that pushes you to grow in that area.

Prompt

What are your core values? How do they align with your daily actions and decisions?

_____

_____

_____

_____

_____

_____

_____

"I honor my values and let them guide me."

ACTION

Write down your top five values. Create an intention for the week to live in alignment with one of those values.

1. _____

_____

_____

2. _____

_____

_____

3. _____

_____

_____

4. _____

_____

_____

5. _____

PRAYER FOR
SELF-LOVE AND
ACCEPTANCE

Scripture Reference
"I am fearfully and wonderfully made." – Psalm 139:14

Prayer Point
Include a prayer to cultivate self-love and acceptance. Acknowledge your inherent worth as a beloved child of God.

Prayer
"Lord, I thank You for the beautiful creation I am. Help me to see myself through Your eyes, with love, grace, and acceptance. Teach me to love and care for myself as You have loved me. Let Your peace surround me as I embrace who I am, and empower me to live authentically and confidently. Amen."

Activation Tip
As you comb your hair or dress for the day, affirm your worth and beauty, recognizing the reflection of God's love in you.

Internalize the Value of Your Value
When you know and accept the value of your value you walk confidently and with purpose because you know your worth and are assured in your abilities and potential. (Excerpt from the book: "Build It Beyond, from a Dream to a Vision for life" Anita Willis, author)

DAY 1

Morning Intention:

What is my intention for today? How will I contribute to my well-being and the well-being of others?

_____

_____

_____

Midday Check-in:

What emotions am I experiencing? What can I do to center myself?

_____

_____

_____

Evening Reflection:

What did I learn today? What did I do to honor myself and others?

_____

_____

_____

DAY 2

Morning Intention:

What is my intention for today? How will I contribute to my well-being and the well-being of others?

_____

_____

_____

Midday Check-in:

What emotions am I experiencing? What can I do to center myself?

_____

_____

_____

Evening Reflection:

What did I learn today? What did I do to honor myself and others?

_____

_____

_____

DAY 3

Morning Intention:

What is my intention for today? How will I contribute to my well-being and the well-being of others?

_____

_____

_____

Midday Check-in:

What emotions am I experiencing? What can I do to center myself?

_____

_____

_____

Evening Reflection:

What did I learn today? What did I do to honor myself and others?

_____

_____

_____

DAY 4

Morning Intention:

What is my intention for today? How will I contribute to my well-being and the well-being of others?

_____

_____

_____

Midday Check-in:

What emotions am I experiencing? What can I do to center myself?

_____

_____

_____

Evening Reflection:

What did I learn today? What did I do to honor myself and others?

_____

_____

_____

DAY 5

Morning Intention:

What is my intention for today? How will I contribute to my well-being and the well-being of others?

_____

_____

_____

Midday Check-in:

What emotions am I experiencing? What can I do to center myself?

_____

_____

_____

Evening Reflection:

What did I learn today? What did I do to honor myself and others?

_____

_____

_____

DAY 6

Morning Intention:

What is my intention for today? How will I contribute to my well-being and the well-being of others?

_____

_____

_____

Midday Check-in:

What emotions am I experiencing? What can I do to center myself?

_____

_____

_____

Evening Reflection:

What did I learn today? What did I do to honor myself and others?

_____

_____

_____

DAY 7

Morning Intention:

What is my intention for today? How will I contribute to my well-being and the well-being of others?

_____

_____

_____

Midday Check-in:

What emotions am I experiencing? What can I do to center myself?

_____

_____

_____

Evening Reflection:

What did I learn today? What did I do to honor myself and others?

_____

_____

_____

Your Thoughts

CULTIVATE EMOTIONAL INTELLIGENCE

Weekly Challenge

Choose one area to deepen your practice: radical self-honesty, emotional intelligence, compassion, or open communication. Set a challenge that pushes you to grow in that area.

Prompt

Recall a recent emotional reaction you had. What was the trigger? How did you handle it?

_____

_____

_____

_____

_____

_____

_____

"I manage my emotions
with grace and patience."

ACTION

Practice mindfulness for 5 minutes daily, focusing on observing your emotions without judgment.

_____

_____

_____

_____

_____

_____

_____

_____

_____

_____

IT IS TIME FOR QUIETUDE

https://youtu.be/v-OCghjGHDo?si=375JkFGHCtgHy3Cb

PRAYER FOR MENTAL CLARITY AND FOCUS

Scripture Reference
"For God gave us a spirit not of fear but of power and love and self-control." - 2 Timothy 1:7

Prayer Point
Ask for clarity and focus in your thoughts, enabling you to make decisions with wisdom and discernment throughout the day.

Prayer
"Heavenly Father, I seek Your guidance and clarity in all that I do today. Help me to focus on what matters most and make decisions that align with Your will for my life. Remove any distractions from my mind and fill me with Your peace and understanding. May I walk in Your wisdom today and always. Amen."

Activation Tip
While washing your face or brushing your hair, reflect on the clarity you need and invite God's wisdom to guide your thoughts.

"Adapt to change by reframing your thoughts"
– by author Anita Wills

DAY 1

Morning Intention:

What is my intention for today? How will I contribute to my well-being and the well-being of others?

_____

_____

_____

Midday Check-in:

What emotions am I experiencing? What can I do to center myself?

_____

_____

_____

Evening Reflection:

What did I learn today? What did I do to honor myself and others?

_____

_____

_____

DAY 2

Morning Intention:

What is my intention for today? How will I contribute to my well-being
and the well-being of others?

_____

_____

_____

Midday Check-in:

What emotions am I experiencing? What can I do to center myself?

_____

_____

_____

Evening Reflection:

What did I learn today? What did I do to honor myself and others?

_____

_____

_____

DAY 3

Morning Intention:

What is my intention for today? How will I contribute to my well-being and the well-being of others?

_____

_____

_____

Midday Check-in:

What emotions am I experiencing? What can I do to center myself?

_____

_____

_____

Evening Reflection:

What did I learn today? What did I do to honor myself and others?

_____

_____

_____

DAY 4

Morning Intention:

What is my intention for today? How will I contribute to my well-being and the well-being of others?

_____

_____

_____

Midday Check-in:

What emotions am I experiencing? What can I do to center myself?

_____

_____

_____

Evening Reflection:

What did I learn today? What did I do to honor myself and others?

_____

_____

_____

DAY 5

Morning Intention:

What is my intention for today? How will I contribute to my well-being and the well-being of others?

_____

_____

_____

Midday Check-in:

What emotions am I experiencing? What can I do to center myself?

_____

_____

_____

Evening Reflection:

What did I learn today? What did I do to honor myself and others?

_____

_____

_____

DAY 6

Morning Intention:

What is my intention for today? How will I contribute to my well-being and the well-being of others?

_____

_____

_____

Midday Check-in:

What emotions am I experiencing? What can I do to center myself?

_____

_____

_____

Evening Reflection:

What did I learn today? What did I do to honor myself and others?

_____

_____

_____

DAY 7

Morning Intention:

What is my intention for today? How will I contribute to my well-being and the well-being of others?

_____

_____

_____

Midday Check-in:

What emotions am I experiencing? What can I do to center myself?

_____

_____

_____

Evening Reflection:

What did I learn today? What did I do to honor myself and others?

_____

_____

_____

Your Thoughts

_____

_____

_____

_____

_____

_____

_____

_____

_____

_____

_____

_____

_____

_____

_____

_____

_____

Week 4

MINDFUL REFLECTION
ON GROWTH

Weekly Challenge

Choose one area to deepen your practice: radical self-honesty, emotional intelligence, compassion, or open communication. Set a challenge that pushes you to grow in that area.

Prompt

Reflect on how you've grown over the past year. What were some challenges you overcame? What lessons did you learn?

_____

_____

_____

_____

_____

_____

_____

AFFIRMATION

"I embrace growth, both in ease and in challenge."

ACTION

Create a "growth map" by identifying key milestones and growth areas for yourself in the past year.

PRAYER FOR
GRATITUDE AND PEACE

Scripture Reference

"Give thanks in all circumstances; for this is the will of God in Christ Jesus for you." – 1 Thessalonians 5:18

Prayer Point

Close each day with a prayer of gratitude. Thank God for the day's blessings, small and large, and ask for His peace to fill your heart and home.

Prayer

"Thank You, Lord, for the gift of this day. I am grateful for Your guidance, Your protection, and Your love. I thank You for the small blessings I often overlook and for the peace You give me in every moment. As I lay down to rest, I ask for Your peace to guard my heart and mind, and for Your presence to renew me. Amen."

Activation Tip

As you prepare for bed, say this prayer as a form of gratitude, reflecting on the day's experiences and closing it with peace and thankfulness.

DAY 1

Morning Intention:

What is my intention for today? How will I contribute to my well-being
and the well-being of others?

_____

_____

_____

Midday Check-in:

What emotions am I experiencing? What can I do to center myself?

_____

_____

_____

Evening Reflection:

What did I learn today? What did I do to honor myself and others?

_____

_____

_____

DAY 2

Morning Intention:

What is my intention for today? How will I contribute to my well-being and the well-being of others?

_____

_____

_____

Midday Check-in:

What emotions am I experiencing? What can I do to center myself?

_____

_____

_____

Evening Reflection:

What did I learn today? What did I do to honor myself and others?

_____

_____

_____

DAY 3

Morning Intention:

What is my intention for today? How will I contribute to my well-being and the well-being of others?

_____

_____

_____

Midday Check-in:

What emotions am I experiencing? What can I do to center myself?

_____

_____

_____

Evening Reflection:

What did I learn today? What did I do to honor myself and others?

_____

_____

_____

DAY 4

Morning Intention:

What is my intention for today? How will I contribute to my well-being and the well-being of others?

_____

_____

_____

Midday Check-in:

What emotions am I experiencing? What can I do to center myself?

_____

_____

_____

Evening Reflection:

What did I learn today? What did I do to honor myself and others?

_____

_____

_____

DAY 5

Morning Intention:

What is my intention for today? How will I contribute to my well-being and the well-being of others?

_____

_____

_____

Midday Check-in:

What emotions am I experiencing? What can I do to center myself?

_____

_____

_____

Evening Reflection:

What did I learn today? What did I do to honor myself and others?

_____

_____

_____

DAY 6

Morning Intention:

What is my intention for today? How will I contribute to my well-being and the well-being of others?

_____

_____

_____

Midday Check-in:

What emotions am I experiencing? What can I do to center myself?

_____

_____

_____

Evening Reflection:

What did I learn today? What did I do to honor myself and others?

_____

_____

_____

DAY 7

Morning Intention:

What is my intention for today? How will I contribute to my well-being and the well-being of others?

_____

_____

_____

Midday Check-in:

What emotions am I experiencing? What can I do to center myself?

_____

_____

_____

Evening Reflection:

What did I learn today? What did I do to honor myself and others?

_____

_____

_____

Your Thoughts

Month 2

Healing from
Disappointment
and Building
Stronger
Relationships

EMBRACE
FORGIVENESS

Weekly Challenge

Choose a relationship-focused challenge: forgiveness, patience, or building stronger bonds. Practice these through small acts each day.

Prompt

Reflect on someone you're holding a grudge against. What would it take for you to release this and forgive?

_____

_____

_____

_____

_____

_____

_____

_____

"I forgive others and myself, knowing that healing begins within."

ACTION

Write a forgiveness letter (you don't have to send it) to release the burden.

_____

_____

_____

_____

_____

_____

_____

_____

_____

_____

_____

FROM I WON'T TO I WELCOME

https://www.tiktok.com/t/ZP8F1QqTj/

PRAYER FOR SELF-FORGIVENESS AND HEALING

Scripture Reference

"For I will restore health to you, and your wounds I will heal, declares the Lord." – Jeremiah 30:17

Prayer Point

Begin each day with a prayer for self-forgiveness and healing. Acknowledge the emotional burdens you carry and ask for divine help in releasing them.

Prayer

"Dear God, I come before You with a heart that seeks healing. I forgive myself for the times I have doubted my worth and allowed my past to define me. Please heal my emotional wounds, renew my spirit, and help me embrace the present moment with peace. Guide me to release any guilt, anger, or pain that I may be carrying and fill me with Your love and grace. Amen."

Activation Tip

As you wash your hands, visualize the cleansing of your spirit, letting go of past hurts and welcoming healing.

DAY 1

Morning Intention:

What is my intention for today? How will I contribute to my well-being and the well-being of others?

_____

_____

_____

Midday Check-in:

What emotions am I experiencing? What can I do to center myself?

_____

_____

_____

Evening Reflection:

What did I learn today? What did I do to honor myself and others?

_____

_____

_____

DAY 2

Morning Intention:

What is my intention for today? How will I contribute to my well-being and the well-being of others?

_____

_____

_____

Midday Check-in:

What emotions am I experiencing? What can I do to center myself?

_____

_____

_____

Evening Reflection:

What did I learn today? What did I do to honor myself and others?

_____

_____

_____

DAY 3

Morning Intention:

What is my intention for today? How will I contribute to my well-being and the well-being of others?

_____

_____

_____

Midday Check-in:

What emotions am I experiencing? What can I do to center myself?

_____

_____

_____

Evening Reflection:

What did I learn today? What did I do to honor myself and others?

_____

_____

_____

DAY 4

Morning Intention:

What is my intention for today? How will I contribute to my well-being and the well-being of others?

_____

_____

_____

Midday Check-in:

What emotions am I experiencing? What can I do to center myself?

_____

_____

_____

Evening Reflection:

What did I learn today? What did I do to honor myself and others?

_____

_____

_____

DAY 5

Morning Intention:

What is my intention for today? How will I contribute to my well-being and the well-being of others?

_____

_____

_____

Midday Check-in:

What emotions am I experiencing? What can I do to center myself?

_____

_____

_____

Evening Reflection:

What did I learn today? What did I do to honor myself and others?

_____

_____

_____

DAY 6

Morning Intention:

What is my intention for today? How will I contribute to my well-being and the well-being of others?

_____

_____

_____

Midday Check-in:

What emotions am I experiencing? What can I do to center myself?

_____

_____

_____

Evening Reflection:

What did I learn today? What did I do to honor myself and others?

_____

_____

_____

DAY 7

Morning Intention:

What is my intention for today? How will I contribute to my well-being and the well-being of others?

_____

_____

_____

Midday Check-in:

What emotions am I experiencing? What can I do to center myself?

_____

_____

_____

Evening Reflection:

What did I learn today? What did I do to honor myself and others?

_____

_____

_____

Your Thoughts

Week 6

CULTIVATE COMPASSION

Weekly Challenge

Choose a relationship-focused challenge: forgiveness, patience, or building stronger bonds. Practice these through small acts each day.

Prompt

Think of a recent interaction where you were frustrated or disappointed. How could you show more compassion in that situation?

_____

_____

_____

_____

_____

_____

_____

_____

"I approach myself and others with compassion and understanding."

ACTION

Practice a random act of kindness each day this week, and observe how it affects your emotions.

_____

_____

_____

_____

_____

_____

_____

_____

_____

_____

MEANINGFUL RELATIONSHIP

https://www.tiktok.com/t/ZP8F101Pu/

PRAYER FOR SELF-LOVE
AND ACCEPTANCE

Scripture Reference
"I am fearfully and wonderfully made." – Psalm 139:14

Prayer Point
Include a prayer to cultivate self-love and acceptance. Acknowledge your inherent worth as a beloved child of God.

Prayer
"Lord, I thank You for the beautiful creation I am. Help me to see myself through Your eyes, with love, grace, and acceptance. Teach me to love and care for myself as You have loved me. Let Your peace surround me as I embrace who I am, and empower me to live authentically and confidently. Amen."

Activation Tip
As you comb your hair or dress for the day, affirm your worth and beauty, recognizing the reflection of God's love in you.

DAY 1

Morning Intention:

What is my intention for today? How will I contribute to my well-being and the well-being of others?

_____

_____

_____

Midday Check-in:

What emotions am I experiencing? What can I do to center myself?

_____

_____

_____

Evening Reflection:

What did I learn today? What did I do to honor myself and others?

_____

_____

_____

DAY 2

Morning Intention:

What is my intention for today? How will I contribute to my well-being and the well-being of others?

_____

_____

_____

Midday Check-in:

What emotions am I experiencing? What can I do to center myself?

_____

_____

_____

Evening Reflection:

What did I learn today? What did I do to honor myself and others?

_____

_____

_____

DAY 3

Morning Intention:

What is my intention for today? How will I contribute to my well-being and the well-being of others?

_____

_____

_____

Midday Check-in:

What emotions am I experiencing? What can I do to center myself?

_____

_____

_____

Evening Reflection:

What did I learn today? What did I do to honor myself and others?

_____

_____

_____

DAY 4

Morning Intention:

What is my intention for today? How will I contribute to my well-being and the well-being of others?

_____

_____

_____

Midday Check-in:

What emotions am I experiencing? What can I do to center myself?

_____

_____

_____

Evening Reflection:

What did I learn today? What did I do to honor myself and others?

_____

_____

_____

DAY 5

Morning Intention:

What is my intention for today? How will I contribute to my well-being and the well-being of others?

_____

_____

_____

Midday Check-in:

What emotions am I experiencing? What can I do to center myself?

_____

_____

_____

Evening Reflection:

What did I learn today? What did I do to honor myself and others?

_____

_____

_____

DAY 6

Morning Intention:

What is my intention for today? How will I contribute to my well-being and the well-being of others?

_____

_____

_____

Midday Check-in:

What emotions am I experiencing? What can I do to center myself?

_____

_____

_____

Evening Reflection:

What did I learn today? What did I do to honor myself and others?

_____

_____

_____

DAY 7

Morning Intention:

What is my intention for today? How will I contribute to my well-being and the well-being of others?

_____

_____

_____

Midday Check-in:

What emotions am I experiencing? What can I do to center myself?

_____

_____

_____

Evening Reflection:

What did I learn today? What did I do to honor myself and others?

_____

_____

_____

Your Thoughts

Week 7

OPEN AND HONEST COMMUNICATION

Weekly Challenge

Choose a relationship-focused challenge: forgiveness, patience, or building stronger bonds. Practice these through small acts each day.

Prompt

How often do you speak openly about your feelings? What makes it difficult?

_____

_____

_____

_____

_____

_____

_____

_____

"I communicate openly,
honestly, and kindly
with others."

ACTION

Have a heart-to-heart conversation with a close friend or loved one about your thoughts and feelings.

_____

_____

_____

_____

_____

_____

_____

_____

_____

_____

_____

YOU ARE EQUIPPED

https://www.tiktok.com/t/ZP8F1qYke/

PRAYER FOR MENTAL CLARITY AND FOCUS

Scripture Reference

"For God gave us a spirit not of fear but of power and love and self-control." - 2 Timothy 1:7

Prayer Point

Ask for clarity and focus in your thoughts, enabling you to make decisions with wisdom and discernment throughout the day.

Prayer

"Heavenly Father, I seek Your guidance and clarity in all that I do today. Help me to focus on what matters most and make decisions that align with Your will for my life. Remove any distractions from my mind and fill me with Your peace and understanding. May I walk in Your wisdom today and always. Amen."

Activation Tip

While washing your face or brushing your hair, reflect on the clarity you need and invite God's wisdom to guide your thoughts.

DAY 1

Morning Intention:

What is my intention for today? How will I contribute to my well-being and the well-being of others?

_____

_____

_____

Midday Check-in:

What emotions am I experiencing? What can I do to center myself?

_____

_____

_____

Evening Reflection:

What did I learn today? What did I do to honor myself and others?

_____

_____

_____

DAY 2

Morning Intention:

What is my intention for today? How will I contribute to my well-being and the well-being of others?

_____

_____

_____

Midday Check-in:

What emotions am I experiencing? What can I do to center myself?

_____

_____

_____

Evening Reflection:

What did I learn today? What did I do to honor myself and others?

_____

_____

_____

DAY 3

Morning Intention:

What is my intention for today? How will I contribute to my well-being and the well-being of others?

_____

_____

_____

Midday Check-in:

What emotions am I experiencing? What can I do to center myself?

_____

_____

_____

Evening Reflection:

What did I learn today? What did I do to honor myself and others?

_____

_____

_____

DAY 4

Morning Intention:

What is my intention for today? How will I contribute to my well-being and the well-being of others?

_____

_____

_____

Midday Check-in:

What emotions am I experiencing? What can I do to center myself?

_____

_____

_____

Evening Reflection:

What did I learn today? What did I do to honor myself and others?

_____

_____

_____

DAY 5

Morning Intention:

What is my intention for today? How will I contribute to my well-being and the well-being of others?

_____

_____

_____

Midday Check-in:

What emotions am I experiencing? What can I do to center myself?

_____

_____

_____

Evening Reflection:

What did I learn today? What did I do to honor myself and others?

_____

_____

_____

Morning Intention:

What is my intention for today? How will I contribute to my well-being and the well-being of others?

_____

_____

_____

Midday Check-in:

What emotions am I experiencing? What can I do to center myself?

_____

_____

_____

Evening Reflection:

What did I learn today? What did I do to honor myself and others?

_____

_____

_____

DAY 7

Morning Intention:

What is my intention for today? How will I contribute to my well-being and the well-being of others?

_____

_____

_____

Midday Check-in:

What emotions am I experiencing? What can I do to center myself?

_____

_____

_____

Evening Reflection:

What did I learn today? What did I do to honor myself and others?

_____

_____

_____

Your Thoughts

_____

_____

_____

_____

_____

_____

_____

_____

_____

_____

_____

_____

_____

_____

_____

_____

_____

_____

Week 8

PATIENCE IN
RELATIONSHIPS

Weekly Challenge

Choose a relationship-focused challenge: forgiveness, patience, or building stronger bonds. Practice these through small acts each day.

Prompt

When was the last time you rushed a decision or interaction in a relationship? What did you learn from it?

_____

_____

_____

_____

_____

_____

_____

_____

"I trust in the timing
of my relationships and
honor their natural flow."

ACTION

Take a step back in a relationship where you may be rushing. Allow time for growth and understanding to unfold.

_____

_____

_____

_____

_____

_____

_____

_____

_____

_____

LUXURY IS NOT COMPLICATED, ELEGANCE TAKES TIME!

https://www.tiktok.com/t/ZP8F1tNJw/

PRAYER FOR STRENGTH AND RESILIENCE

Scripture Reference

"I can do all things through Christ who strengthens me."

- Philippians 4:13

Prayer Point

Include a prayer for strength as you prepare for the challenges of the day. Ask for resilience in handling life's difficulties and to maintain a positive mindset.

Prayer

"Lord, I ask for Your strength today. Equip me with the resilience to face every challenge and the courage to remain steadfast in my journey. No matter what comes my way, I trust in Your power to guide me. Fill me with the strength I need to push forward with a hopeful heart and a focused mind. Amen."

Activation Tip

While brushing your teeth or applying skincare, take a moment to mentally and spiritually "armor up," preparing yourself for the day ahead with strength and faith.

DAY 1

Morning Intention:

What is my intention for today? How will I contribute to my well-being and the well-being of others?

_____

_____

_____

Midday Check-in:

What emotions am I experiencing? What can I do to center myself?

_____

_____

_____

Evening Reflection:

What did I learn today? What did I do to honor myself and others?

_____

_____

_____

DAY 2

Morning Intention:

What is my intention for today? How will I contribute to my well-being and the well-being of others?

_____

_____

_____

Midday Check-in:

What emotions am I experiencing? What can I do to center myself?

_____

_____

_____

Evening Reflection:

What did I learn today? What did I do to honor myself and others?

_____

_____

_____

DAY 3

Morning Intention:

What is my intention for today? How will I contribute to my well-being and the well-being of others?

_____

_____

_____

Midday Check-in:

What emotions am I experiencing? What can I do to center myself?

_____

_____

_____

Evening Reflection:

What did I learn today? What did I do to honor myself and others?

_____

_____

_____

DAY 4

Morning Intention:

What is my intention for today? How will I contribute to my well-being and the well-being of others?

_____

_____

_____

Midday Check-in:

What emotions am I experiencing? What can I do to center myself?

_____

_____

_____

Evening Reflection:

What did I learn today? What did I do to honor myself and others?

_____

_____

_____

DAY 5

Morning Intention:

What is my intention for today? How will I contribute to my well-being and the well-being of others?

_____

_____

_____

Midday Check-in:

What emotions am I experiencing? What can I do to center myself?

_____

_____

_____

Evening Reflection:

What did I learn today? What did I do to honor myself and others?

_____

_____

_____

DAY 6

Morning Intention:

What is my intention for today? How will I contribute to my well-being and the well-being of others?

_____

_____

_____

Midday Check-in:

What emotions am I experiencing? What can I do to center myself?

_____

_____

_____

Evening Reflection:

What did I learn today? What did I do to honor myself and others?

_____

_____

_____

DAY 7

Morning Intention:

What is my intention for today? How will I contribute to my well-being and the well-being of others?

_____

_____

_____

Midday Check-in:

What emotions am I experiencing? What can I do to center myself?

_____

_____

_____

Evening Reflection:

What did I learn today? What did I do to honor myself and others?

_____

_____

_____

Your Thoughts

Month 3

Renewal, Strengthening Connections, and Vision for the Future

Week 9

REAFFIRM YOUR
COMMITMENT TO YOURSELF

Weekly Challenge

Focus on renewal and creating your vision. Write down your goals and map out your steps to achieve them.

Prompt

How do you show commitment to yourself? How has this practice supported you in the past?

_____

_____

_____

_____

_____

_____

_____

_____

"I am committed
to my well-being,
growth, and future."

ACTION

Write down one personal goal that aligns with your values and commit to it for the next three months.

_____

_____

_____

_____

_____

_____

_____

_____

_____

_____

_____

_____

_____

PRAYER FOR SELF-LOVE
AND ACCEPTANCE

Scripture Reference
"I am fearfully and wonderfully made." – Psalm 139:14

Prayer Point
Include a prayer to cultivate self-love and acceptance. Acknowledge your inherent worth as a beloved child of God.

Prayer
"Lord, I thank You for the beautiful creation I am. Help me to see myself through Your eyes, with love, grace, and acceptance. Teach me to love and care for myself as You have loved me. Let Your peace surround me as I embrace who I am, and empower me to live authentically and confidently. Amen."

Activation Tip
As you comb your hair or dress for the day, affirm your worth and beauty, recognizing the reflection of God's love in you.

DAY 1

Morning Intention:

What is my intention for today? How will I contribute to my well-being and the well-being of others?

_____

_____

_____

Midday Check-in:

What emotions am I experiencing? What can I do to center myself?

_____

_____

_____

Evening Reflection:

What did I learn today? What did I do to honor myself and others?

_____

_____

_____

Morning Intention:

What is my intention for today? How will I contribute to my well-being and the well-being of others?

_____

_____

_____

Midday Check-in:

What emotions am I experiencing? What can I do to center myself?

_____

_____

_____

Evening Reflection:

What did I learn today? What did I do to honor myself and others?

_____

_____

_____

DAY 3

Morning Intention:

What is my intention for today? How will I contribute to my well-being and the well-being of others?

_____

_____

_____

Midday Check-in:

What emotions am I experiencing? What can I do to center myself?

_____

_____

_____

Evening Reflection:

What did I learn today? What did I do to honor myself and others?

_____

_____

_____

DAY 4

Morning Intention:

What is my intention for today? How will I contribute to my well-being and the well-being of others?

_____

_____

_____

Midday Check-in:

What emotions am I experiencing? What can I do to center myself?

_____

_____

_____

Evening Reflection:

What did I learn today? What did I do to honor myself and others?

_____

_____

_____

DAY 5

Morning Intention:

What is my intention for today? How will I contribute to my well-being and the well-being of others?

_____

_____

_____

Midday Check-in:

What emotions am I experiencing? What can I do to center myself?

_____

_____

_____

Evening Reflection:

What did I learn today? What did I do to honor myself and others?

_____

_____

_____

DAY 6

Morning Intention:

What is my intention for today? How will I contribute to my well-being and the well-being of others?

_____

_____

_____

Midday Check-in:

What emotions am I experiencing? What can I do to center myself?

_____

_____

_____

Evening Reflection:

What did I learn today? What did I do to honor myself and others?

_____

_____

_____

DAY 7

Morning Intention:

What is my intention for today? How will I contribute to my well-being and the well-being of others?

_____

_____

_____

Midday Check-in:

What emotions am I experiencing? What can I do to center myself?

_____

_____

_____

Evening Reflection:

What did I learn today? What did I do to honor myself and others?

_____

_____

_____

Your Thoughts

Week 10

GRATITUDE AS A HEALING PRACTICE

Weekly Challenge

Focus on renewal and creating your vision. Write down your goals and map out your steps to achieve them.

Prompt

What are you most grateful for right now? Reflect on how practicing gratitude has transformed your mindset.

_____

_____

_____

_____

_____

_____

_____

_____

AFFIRMATION

"I am thankful for
the present moment
and the blessings
within it."

ACTION

Start a gratitude list. Write down 3 things you are grateful for each day.

_____

_____

_____

_____

_____

_____

_____

_____

_____

_____

_____

_____

INHALE AND RELEASE...YOU ARE WORTHY

https://www.tiktok.com/t/ZP8F10ugf/

PRAYER FOR GRATITUDE AND PEACE

Scripture Reference

"Give thanks in all circumstances; for this is the will of God in Christ Jesus for you." - 1 Thessalonians 5:18

Prayer Point

Close each day with a prayer of gratitude. Thank God for the day's blessings, small and large, and ask for His peace to fill your heart and home.

Prayer

"Thank You, Lord, for the gift of this day. I am grateful for Your guidance, Your protection, and Your love. I thank You for the small blessings I often overlook and for the peace You give me in every moment. As I lay down to rest I ask for Your peace to guard my heart and mind, and for Your presence to renew me. Amen."

Activation Tip

As you prepare for bed, say this prayer as a form of gratitude, reflecting on the day's experiences and closing it with peace and thankfulness.

DAY 1

Morning Intention:

What is my intention for today? How will I contribute to my well-being and the well-being of others?

_____

_____

_____

Midday Check-in:

What emotions am I experiencing? What can I do to center myself?

_____

_____

_____

Evening Reflection:

What did I learn today? What did I do to honor myself and others?

_____

_____

_____

DAY 2

Morning Intention:

What is my intention for today? How will I contribute to my well-being and the well-being of others?

_____

_____

_____

Midday Check-in:

What emotions am I experiencing? What can I do to center myself?

_____

_____

_____

Evening Reflection:

What did I learn today? What did I do to honor myself and others?

_____

_____

_____

DAY 3

Morning Intention:

What is my intention for today? How will I contribute to my well-being and the well-being of others?

_____

_____

_____

Midday Check-in:

What emotions am I experiencing? What can I do to center myself?

_____

_____

_____

Evening Reflection:

What did I learn today? What did I do to honor myself and others?

_____

_____

_____

DAY 4

Morning Intention:

What is my intention for today? How will I contribute to my well-being and the well-being of others?

_____

_____

_____

Midday Check-in:

What emotions am I experiencing? What can I do to center myself?

_____

_____

_____

Evening Reflection:

What did I learn today? What did I do to honor myself and others?

_____

_____

_____

DAY 5

Morning Intention:

What is my intention for today? How will I contribute to my well-being and the well-being of others?

_____

_____

_____

Midday Check-in:

What emotions am I experiencing? What can I do to center myself?

_____

_____

_____

Evening Reflection:

What did I learn today? What did I do to honor myself and others?

_____

_____

_____

DAY 6

Morning Intention:

What is my intention for today? How will I contribute to my well-being and the well-being of others?

_____

_____

_____

Midday Check-in:

What emotions am I experiencing? What can I do to center myself?

_____

_____

_____

Evening Reflection:

What did I learn today? What did I do to honor myself and others?

_____

_____

_____

DAY 7

Morning Intention:

What is my intention for today? How will I contribute to my well-being and the well-being of others?

_____

_____

_____

Midday Check-in:

What emotions am I experiencing? What can I do to center myself?

_____

_____

_____

Evening Reflection:

What did I learn today? What did I do to honor myself and others?

_____

_____

_____

Your Thoughts

Week 11

FOCUS ON COLLABORATION AND COMMUNITY

Weekly Challenge

Focus on renewal and creating your vision. Write down your goals and map out your steps to achieve them.

Prompt

Think about a community or group you are part of. How can you contribute more to strengthen that bond?

_____

_____

_____

_____

_____

_____

_____

_____

"I contribute my energy and talents to foster connection and collaboration."

ACTION

Volunteer or take a step to connect with others in a community setting.

_____

_____

_____

_____

_____

_____

_____

_____

_____

_____

_____

_____

FASHION CHALLENGE

Now that you have made it to "Week 11", take a before and after picture
that reflects how your personal fashion presentation has increased .

PRAYER FOR STRENGTH AND RESILIENCE

Scripture Reference
"I can do all things through Christ who strengthens me."
- Philippians 4:13

Prayer Point
Include a prayer for strength as you prepare for the challenges of the day. Ask for resilience in handling life's difficulties and to maintain a positive mindset.

Prayer
"Lord, I ask for Your strength today. Equip me with the resilience to face every challenge and the courage to remain steadfast in my journey. No matter what comes my way, I trust in Your power to guide me. Fill me with the strength I need to push forward with a hopeful heart and a focused mind. Amen."

Activation Tip
While brushing your teeth or applying skincare, take a moment to mentally and spiritually "armor up," preparing yourself for the day ahead with strength and faith.

DAY 1

Morning Intention:

What is my intention for today? How will I contribute to my well-being and the well-being of others?

_____

_____

_____

Midday Check-in:

What emotions am I experiencing? What can I do to center myself?

_____

_____

_____

Evening Reflection:

What did I learn today? What did I do to honor myself and others?

_____

_____

_____

DAY 2

Morning Intention:

What is my intention for today? How will I contribute to my well-being and the well-being of others?

_____

_____

_____

Midday Check-in:

What emotions am I experiencing? What can I do to center myself?

_____

_____

_____

Evening Reflection:

What did I learn today? What did I do to honor myself and others?

_____

_____

_____

DAY 3

Morning Intention:

What is my intention for today? How will I contribute to my well-being and the well-being of others?

_____

_____

_____

Midday Check-in:

What emotions am I experiencing? What can I do to center myself?

_____

_____

_____

Evening Reflection:

What did I learn today? What did I do to honor myself and others?

_____

_____

_____

DAY 4

Morning Intention:

What is my intention for today? How will I contribute to my well-being and the well-being of others?

_____

_____

_____

Midday Check-in:

What emotions am I experiencing? What can I do to center myself?

_____

_____

_____

Evening Reflection:

What did I learn today? What did I do to honor myself and others?

_____

_____

_____

DAY 5

Morning Intention:

What is my intention for today? How will I contribute to my well-being
and the well-being of others?

_____

_____

_____

Midday Check-in:

What emotions am I experiencing? What can I do to center myself?

_____

_____

_____

Evening Reflection:

What did I learn today? What did I do to honor myself and others?

_____

_____

_____

DAY 6

Morning Intention:

What is my intention for today? How will I contribute to my well-being and the well-being of others?

_____

_____

_____

Midday Check-in:

What emotions am I experiencing? What can I do to center myself?

_____

_____

_____

Evening Reflection:

What did I learn today? What did I do to honor myself and others?

_____

_____

_____

DAY 7

Morning Intention:

What is my intention for today? How will I contribute to my well-being and the well-being of others?

_____

_____

_____

Midday Check-in:

What emotions am I experiencing? What can I do to center myself?

_____

_____

_____

Evening Reflection:

What did I learn today? What did I do to honor myself and others?

_____

_____

_____

Your Thoughts

Week 12

SETTING INTENTIONS FOR THE FUTURE

Weekly Challenge

Focus on renewal and creating your vision. Write down your goals and map out your steps to achieve them.

Prompt

What do you envision for yourself in the next 6 months? What intentions can you set to align your actions with your vision?

_____

_____

_____

_____

_____

_____

_____

_____

"I create a future of
abundance, love,
and purpose."

ACTION

Write down your vision for the next year and break it down into actionable goals for the next month.

_____

_____

_____

_____

_____

_____

_____

_____

_____

_____

_____

FASHION CHALLENGE

Now that you have made it to "Week 12", take a before and after picture that reflects how your personal fashion presentation has increased .

PRAYER FOR STRENGTH
AND RESILIENCE

Scripture Reference

"I can do all things through Christ who strengthens me."
- Philippians 4:13

Prayer Point

Include a prayer for strength as you prepare for the challenges of the day. Ask for resilience in handling life's difficulties and to maintain a positive mindset.

Prayer

"Lord, I ask for Your strength today. Equip me with the resilience to face every challenge and the courage to remain steadfast in my journey. No matter what comes my way, I trust in Your power to guide me. Fill me with the strength I need to push forward with a hopeful heart and a focused mind. Amen."

Activation Tip

While brushing your teeth or applying skincare, take a moment to mentally and spiritually "armor up," preparing yourself for the day ahead with strength and faith.

DAY 1

Morning Intention:

What is my intention for today? How will I contribute to my well-being and the well-being of others?

_____

_____

_____

Midday Check-in:

What emotions am I experiencing? What can I do to center myself?

_____

_____

_____

Evening Reflection:

What did I learn today? What did I do to honor myself and others?

_____

_____

_____

DAY 2

Morning Intention:

What is my intention for today? How will I contribute to my well-being and the well-being of others?

_____

_____

_____

Midday Check-in:

What emotions am I experiencing? What can I do to center myself?

_____

_____

_____

Evening Reflection:

What did I learn today? What did I do to honor myself and others?

_____

_____

_____

DAY 3

Morning Intention:

What is my intention for today? How will I contribute to my well-being and the well-being of others?

_____

_____

_____

Midday Check-in:

What emotions am I experiencing? What can I do to center myself?

_____

_____

_____

Evening Reflection:

What did I learn today? What did I do to honor myself and others?

_____

_____

_____

DAY 4

Morning Intention:

What is my intention for today? How will I contribute to my well-being and the well-being of others?

_____

_____

_____

Midday Check-in:

What emotions am I experiencing? What can I do to center myself?

_____

_____

_____

Evening Reflection:

What did I learn today? What did I do to honor myself and others?

_____

_____

_____

DAY 5

Morning Intention:

What is my intention for today? How will I contribute to my well-being
and the well-being of others?

_____

_____

_____

Midday Check-in:

What emotions am I experiencing? What can I do to center myself?

_____

_____

_____

Evening Reflection:

What did I learn today? What did I do to honor myself and others?

_____

_____

_____

DAY 6

Morning Intention:

What is my intention for today? How will I contribute to my well-being and the well-being of others?

_____

_____

_____

Midday Check-in:

What emotions am I experiencing? What can I do to center myself?

_____

_____

_____

Evening Reflection:

What did I learn today? What did I do to honor myself and others?

_____

_____

_____

DAY 7

Morning Intention:

What is my intention for today? How will I contribute to my well-being and the well-being of others?

_____

_____

_____

Midday Check-in:

What emotions am I experiencing? What can I do to center myself?

_____

_____

_____

Evening Reflection:

What did I learn today? What did I do to honor myself and others?

_____

_____

_____

Closing Thoughts

As you step into, may you continue to build a deeper understanding of yourself and others. Remember, healing from disappointment is not about erasing the past, but learning from it and moving forward with resilience and compassion. May your journey this year be filled with growth, connection, and the loving participation in the life you are creating.

This journal is designed to help you step into the new year with intention, gratitude, and the mindset necessary to navigate disappointments, strengthen relationships, and embrace personal growth. Each practice encourages mindful reflection and active action toward creating a fulfilling, loving, and collaborative life.

YOUR EBENEZER MOMENT

https://www.tiktok.com/t/ZP8F1c4oH/

The next 90 days will be about transitioning from awareness to active transformation. It's about deepening your connection with yourself and others while embracing the challenges and opportunities that arise along the way. By focusing on intention-setting, resilience, emotional intelligence, and strengthening relationships, you'll create a solid foundation for ongoing personal growth in the new year. The journey ahead is about taking small, intentional steps each day that lead to profound, lasting change.

This progression ensures that, after completing the first 90-day journal, you can now actively build on your past achievements while embarking on an empowered, intentional path toward your best self. The focus will be reflective and action-oriented, creating a harmonious blend of growth, mindfulness, affirming, and transformational wellness. Register now for Part 2 in the IBH Awareness Series, this is our "Sound of Love".

Email request to: media@builditbeyond.com to be notified when the journal is ready for purchase.

VIRTUAL SWAG
Exclusive for Journal Owners Only

Be the First to be notified about our **IBH Destination Coaching Retreats!** We want to meet you! Request more information at: media@builditbeyond.com

- IBH Destination Retreats
- 1x1 Personal Retreats
- 2-4 Group Retreats
- 6-10 Group Retreats
- https://IBHCoachingRetreats.now.site

Temperament Coaching & Consultation Offer exclusively with purchase of the IBH 90 Day Awareness Journal (for proof of purchase you must send a picture with the journal).

Email request and proof of purchase to: media@builditbeyond.com
REQUEST TEMPERAMENT INTRO OFFER in the subject.

Newsletter: Wellness Tips and Treats

Enjoy our virtual newsletter that offers tips and treats shared by colleagues of Anita! "I know you will enjoy the information shared by a few of our facilitators who partner with the IBH Destination Coaching Retreats. Get to know them and enjoy a few introductory offers exclusively for those who purchase this wonderful journal series."

Email for more information:
Subject: Wellness Tips and Treats:
media@builditbeyond.com

SPECIAL NOTE FROM ANITA

A heartfelt shoutout to the incredible professionals joining us in our upcoming virtual newsletter! They're bringing you an exclusive mix of beauty tips and uplifting encouragement, all packed into our virtual swag bag.

Each one has generously pledged their support to our nonprofit, IBH Sister Sounds World. We're thrilled to invite you to discover more about our mission to serve communities both in the United States and Harare, Zimbabwe.

Join us in this journey of giving, learning, and growing together.

Learn more at
BuildItBeyondCoaching.now.site

Meet Anita

There will be times in your life when you find yourself unsatisfied with where you are. You feel like somethings got to change, but you're unsure of where to begin. Here we are starting over and you are convinced that you will not go any further until you're fully resolved to go forward and never look back. Awareness means to have knowledge or perception of a situation or fact.

How do you move forward aware of your strengths and how to strengthen your weaknesses. As stated in the book I've written, Build It Beyond, from a dream to a vision for life, transformation begins with your core values; it blossoms when you se your value to guide your decisions and actions.

I propose that the time to take action is now! No more New year resolutions without clarifying your resolve. Your decision to move forward belongs solely to you. This 90 Awareness Journal is the first step in a series of 4 transformational journals that will support leading you into the honest truth about your growth and development. In other words, you will establish for yourself a personal resolve to learn what it takes for you to celebrate your strengths and with great intentionality address the thoughts, words and behaviors that hold you back.

I know in a very personal way how facing the woman or man in the mirror creates opportunities for creativity and prosperity. The IBH New Year Guided Awareness Journal is not just a tool for reflection; it supports a self-directed transformational companion for women on the journey to personal and professional growth. I am passionate about affirming care, resilience and a grounded sens of self, while aligning with the deeper spiritual values ad truth in our existence. Of course, in no way is this therapy, formal consultation or professional advice, but as information that you can consider at your discretion what is important to your growth, spirit, soul and body.

Speaker, author trainer, and lifestyle/temperament coach, Anita Willis is the force behind IBH Group and IBH Sister Sounds World a non-profit organization. Anita has spent a lifetime encouraging others to live with authenticity, transparency, faith , courage, beauty and confidence. He social media platforms are known for inspiring and encouraging women to take action concerning their self-care spirit, soul and body.

Her experience as an image enhancement professional, ordained minister, mother, grand mother and accomplished scholar, having earned a master's degree in leadership, Host of Destination Coaching Retreats, Anita has learned to leverage challenging experiences to curate an arsenal of wisdom that is practically applied as a Temperament Leadership Coach. With faith and resilience, she embraces her vision and value and encourages other to be authentic powerful, loving and grateful.

CONTACT:
Virtual & Live Speaking Engagements
anitawillis@builditbeyond.com